Michal Ronnen Safdie

With an introduction by

Yehuda Amichai

THE WESTERN WALL

HUGH LAUTER LEVIN ASSOCIATES, INC.

© 1997 Hugh Lauter Levin Associates, Inc.

Design by Philip Grushkin

Photographs © Michal Ronnen Safdie

Printed in Hong Kong

ISBN 0-88363-197-0

CONTENTS

For MOSHE

Whose eye enriched my own.

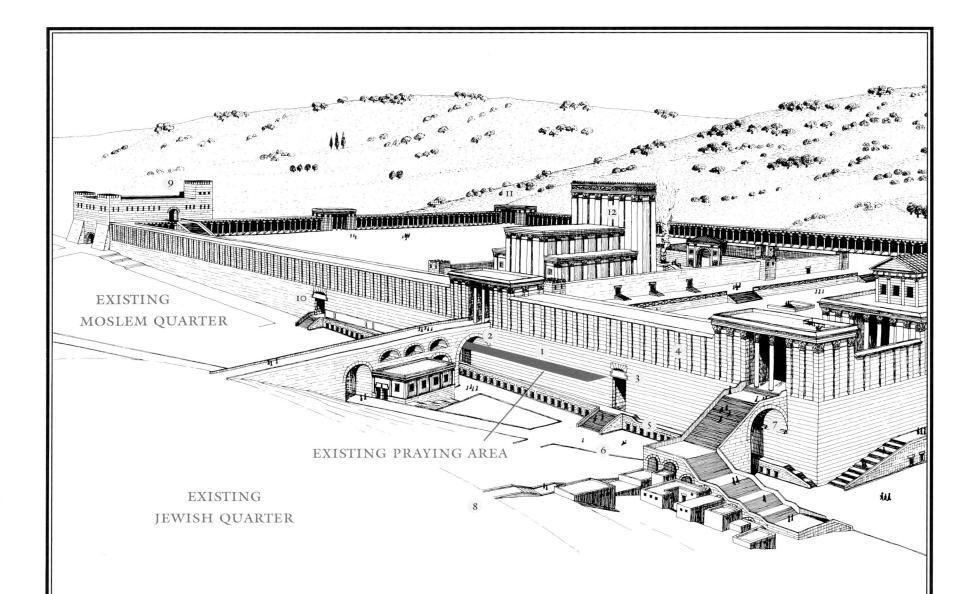

EXISTING
MOSLEM QUARTER

EXISTING PRAYING AREA

EXISTING
JEWISH QUARTER

THE TEMPLE MOUNT *During the Second Temple Period*

DETAIL OF A RECONSTRUCTION BASED ON ARCHAEOLOGICAL AND HISTORICAL EVIDENCE

1. WESTERN WALL

2. WILSON'S ARCH

3. BARCLAY'S GATE

4. PILASTERS

5. SMALL SHOPS

6. MAIN N-S STREET

7. ROBINSON'S ARCH

8. UPPER CITY

9. ANTONIA FORTRESS

10. WARREN'S GATE

11. HERODIAN TOWER

12. THE SECOND TEMPLE

WHEN I FIRST VIEWED this abundance of photographs, I asked myself if this unique and most exciting book needed an introduction—or any commentary at all. This book instantly compels you to enter a whole world of language—body language, color language, stone language, and soul language. The artist set out to do her work without any preconception, whether religious, historical, or emotional. It is this seeming attachment and detachment that makes this book both very personal and very universal. The hands, colors, faces, clothes, masses, and stones are alive and tell us an enthralling story, a deep narrative.

Another question emerges. What if this book (I call it *book* and not *album*) reaches someone far away who knows nothing about Jews and Judaism and the Holy Land and Jerusalem and the Temple twice destroyed? I am quite sure that even this person will feel the pulse of a great dramatic story being told—something of primal holiness, some kind of a great pre-cultic human movement and formation, the very material out of which religions come into being.

Yet I feel the need to write a short historical introduction. What have all these images in common? What makes

them move together? It is that each photograph contains the whole story. Together, they're like a mosaic. But unlike a mosaic, each single, square picture-stone can be viewed independently and has in it holiness and profanity, happiness and sadness, belief and down-to-earth life, eternity and mortality, all together with no beginning and no end.

Writing the story of the Western Wall is more like writing a biography. *Bio* means life. So this will be a short life story of someone who is still alive. You won't be able to sum up or reach conclusions as in history or archaeology. This Wall is still alive because the people in front of it are alive. Sometimes the people are the soul of the Wall, and sometimes the Wall is the soul of the people.

The Wall is actually the western retaining wall surrounding the Temple that was built by Herod. The Temple was destroyed twice—first, by the Babylonians in 586 B.C.E. and later by the Romans in 70 C.E. Jews went on calling it the Western Wall. The more romantic and dramatic or almost journalistic names are "Wailing Wall," "Wall of Tears," or "Wall of Lamentations." At the Western Wall, Jews remember the Temple and pray for the third Temple, heralded by the arrival of the Messiah (calling it "Third House"), but also bring to the Wall their most personal grievances and joys. This is one of the holiest sites Jews have. Christians and Moslems, for whom Jerusalem is also holy, have other places of devotion—Rome and Mecca and Medina. And it is this fact

The remains of ancient shop fronts and public buildings along the Herodian (Second Temple) street.

that brings us to the heart of the Jerusalem problem, a theological and historical and, alas, political problem all at once.

Why Jerusalem? There are cities more beautiful in the world, higher cities, more centrally located beside mighty rivers or beautiful oceans. There must be some strange appeal to a place if it is to attract religion, some kind of God-appeal. We may never know the answer—it may be up in the heavenly universe or far in the past with the creation of the Earth. Conquerors and lovers, God seekers and hope seekers, war seekers and peace seekers, all come to Jerusalem to be redeemed if only for a short while.

King Solomon built the First Temple. It was sacked and the Jews were exiled to Babylonia in 586 B.C.E. Jews began to return to Jerusalem in waves, beginning in 539 B.C.E. The Second Temple, without the magnificent ren-

An archaeological dig at the southern part of the Wall.

ovations later added by King Herod, and lacking the splendor of the earlier Solomonic one, began in 516 B.C.E.

Around 168 B.C.E. the Temple was desecrated again by the Greeks and Syrians. King Herod, the Roman vassal king, rebuilt it in 37 B.C.E., a glorious achievement for the ambitious king. But in 70 C.E., the Emperor Titus burned the Temple to the ground and the Jewish state came to an end. In the 4th century, under Byzantine rule, Jerusalem became a Christian city. Pilgrims flocked to it to visit places relating to the advent of Christianity. In 638, the Caliph Omar conquered the city, and in 691, the Moslems built the octagonal mosque known today as the Dome of the Rock on the site of the Jewish Temple. Here is where, according to Jewish tradition, Adam is buried and God tested Abraham's faith. Here also the Holy of Holies once stood. Moslems believe that Ishmael was almost sacrificed at this site and that the mosque enshrines the rock from which Mohammed ascended to Heaven.

In 1099, Jerusalem became the capital of the Latin Kingdom after being conquered by the Crusaders, who massacred most of the Jewish and Moslem inhabitants. Then in 1187 Saladin took Jerusalem. About seven centuries of Moslem rule followed. The city became neglected and backward and the population decreased, with the exception of the Mameluke period (1250–1517), which saw a burgeoning of arts and culture. Whatever the ruling government, there were always Jews who remained in Jerusalem. Memory and hope made them constant witnesses to the fate of the city. Only in the 16th century did Jerusalem recover and regain some of its former splendor. Backwardness slowly began to give way to European progress. By the middle of the 19th century, the number of inhabitants had increased, half of them Jews.

In 1917, General Allenby rode to the Old City in command of the British and Allied armies and in 1920 set up

An intact drainage system along the curb of the Herodian street.

the British Mandate to replace the Ottoman rule. During the thirty years under the British, Jerusalem was transformed into a thriving city. One of the great things that happened was the law set up by Sir Ronald Storres, Military Governor of Jerusalem, which required that houses in Jerusalem be built only with natural stones, and so every house looked almost like a little replica of the Western Wall.

In the War of Independence, in 1948, the Jewish Quarter, one of the four ethnocentric divisions of Jerusalem (the others being Moslem, Christian, and Armenian) that developed over the centuries, was destroyed and its population forced to leave by the Jordanian-Palestinian conquerors. For nineteen years, during the Arab occupation, Jews were not permitted to visit their holiest place, the Western Wall. During this period of the divided city, Mount Zion, to the southwest of the Old City, became a kind of substitute for the Western Wall. People prayed from there in the direction of the Wall and tried to imagine it hidden deep below the gold Dome of the Rock. So now the Wall, which itself is a substitute for the Temple, was substituted by Mount Zion, adding more distance to the already stretched memory and longing.

I remember Robert Frost's visit to Jerusalem in the 1950s. As a U.S. citizen, he could easily move between the

Detail of a stereoscopic image of the Western Wall, taken c. 1910–1920. Keystone Co. Courtesy of Dan Kyram.

Mass prayer of religious nationalists following a terrorist attack.

two parts of the city. At a party at the Hebrew University, we all, almost before talking literature, asked him about the Jewish Quarter and had he been at the Western Wall? He gladly agreed to describe it very exactly as only poets can describe. I wish I had taped him.

So, Jerusalem was conquered by many, and each conqueror became her lover and left buildings, like jewelry bestowed on a woman. Roman, Byzantine, Arab, Cru-

sader, Russian, Italian, and German and British-styled buildings are all over the city. But her most constant lover, the Jewish people, left only this gray wall as an eternal gift of love.

Until 1967, Jews had only a narrow strip in front of the Wall that lay in the Moslem quarter. And there was at all times humiliation and deprivation and harassment as the Jews made their way to this Moslem section to pray at this holy site. There were the Arab riots in 1921 and 1929 and in 1936-1939 under the leadership of the Grand Mufti Haj Amin el Hussein, who later cooperated openly with Nazi Germany. I remember that sometimes, when I went with my father to pray at the Wall, we had stones hurled at us.

Since 1967, the Western Wall has been fronted by a large plaza. In 1967, the Jewish Quarter was expanded into what was then a Moslem neighborhood that abuts this section of the Wall. A small Moslem neighborhood was demolished and replaced by the existing plaza. At the eastern side, it is like a commitment to memory. Jews keep the memory of their land wherever they are. For example, they keep the prayer for rain in autumn even when praying in different climates. To give you an American example, Jews in Seattle will pray in October for rain with all their hearts and with mighty voices even though, outside the synagogue, it is raining heavily.

Again we have this strange mixture of reality and dreamlike memory. But unlike the prayer, the Western Wall is solid reality—a memory made of stone. In Jewish homes all over the world there are many more pictures and photographs of the Wall than there are paintings of the imagined architecture of the Temple.

There are numerous stories, both real and legendary, about this place. I'll mention just a few at random. After the destruction of the Second Temple by the Romans, four great sages, Gamaliel, Eleazar, Yoshua, and Akiva, returned and viewed the ruins from Mount Scopus. They saw a fox leaving the site of the Holy of Holies and they started to cry, saddened that this holy place should be violated by the wanderings of wild animals. Rabbi Akiva, however, laughed. "Akiva! We are weeping, and you laugh!" the others said to him. "If God is so generous to the idolaters who anger him," Akiva answered, "how

much more to those who do His will!" Akiva is referring to the prophecy of the presence of a fox at the Holy of Holies; since that prophecy came to pass, so will the rebuilding of the Temple, which was also prophesied.

Rabbi Elijah, the Talmudic scholar, evoking the famous dream of Jacob, wrote: "I so much long to ascend God's mountain and the gate of Heaven, and behold, I saw a ladder reaching from the ground [of the Western Wall] and its top in Heaven."

In 392 C.E., Hieronymus, known to Christians as St. Jerome, a scholar who lived in Jerusalem and wrote prolifically on the Old Testament, reflected in his commentary to the Book of Zephaniah (a minor Old Testament prophet), "There they stand [at the Wall], their eyes overflowing with tears, their hands trembling and their hair wild, and the guards demand money to permit them to weep and lament."

Yehuda Halevi, the most famous poet of the Middle Ages, lived in the southern part of Spain about a thousand years ago, at a time when Jews and Moslems were living together in peace, sharing the arts, the sciences, poetry, and riches. Halevi was much acclaimed by Jews and non-Jews. He was a celebrity and lived a splendid life. But despite all this, the opening line of one of his poems reads, "My heart is in the East, but I myself am at the far end of the West," which is an immensely romantic expression of human longing for the unreachable. But this great man went beyond yearning and longing and broke the code of romanticism and frustration. He left his home and his life of fame and riches and sailed to the Holy land.

*Moslem women praying outside of the Dome of the Rock, under the watchful
eye of Israeli soldiers and police during Friday Ramadan prayers.*

In those days, sailing was a very long and dangerous endeavor. Legend has it that Rabbi Yehuda finally reached the Western Wall and was slain by a Saracen horseman while touching the stones in prayer. In reality, he came as far as Alexandria in Egypt, but died there of heart disease.

Another famous Jewish traveler, Benjamin of Tudela, whose aim it was to find the lost Jewish people, wrote in 1170: "One of the walls is the western outer wall of the Temple and they call it 'Gate of Mercy.'" (What a wonderful idea to call a gateless wall "Gate of Mercy"!)

In 1543, Rabbi David wrote in his interpretation of the Song of Songs, that wonderful book of love songs (which the sages say describe the love of God for Israel): "God is not happy at all at the places he used to dwell: the Burning Bush, Mount Sinai, or even the Holy Tabernacle. Only when He'll be a layer of the Western Wall will He be happy, as it is written in the Song of Songs, 'There He is standing behind the Wall.'"

The last two Wall stories bring us into our time. Moslems and later the British (for political reasons) issued many restrictions concerning the narrow strip in front of the Wall. One of them forbade Jews to sound the *shofar* (ram's horn) during the High Holy days. So each year an underground group called *Plugat Hakotel* (Wall Brigade) made it their task to sound at least one note. It became a kind of game when the British police tried, in vain, to prevent it. Some of the Wall Brigade people were always arrested.

My own experience happened only a few years ago. On a Yom Kippur day at dusk, the huge plaza was filled with worshippers for the last prayer, "Open for us the gates, even as they are closing. The day is waning, the sun is low. The hour is late, a year has slipped away. Let us enter the gates at last." And in the deep silence of the masses there suddenly was the sound of the *shofar*. A very weak sound it was, not the wild and loud blowing of the horn. But this weak sound was like the first cry of a new-born baby.

People who come to the Wall for the first time are always amazed and sometimes even disappointed. Is this the holiest place for the Jews? The plaza is sometimes filled with people moving around in aimless, chaotic ways. There are weddings, bar mitzvah celebrations, ethnic ceremonies, and here and there tourist groups and even demonstrations and colorfully dressed individuals. From above, it seems like a modern ballet or even more like a busy airport, with noises and voices and questions

and directions and groups and lost individuals and carry-on bags and cameras. And from time to time you can hear the muezzins chanting from their minarets and the church bells and public announcements. There are meeting points at the southern entrance and at the tunnel entrance and at the big stairs. And, as in a real airport, all this strange movement comes to a more or less ordered end or a new beginning at the gates. The Western Wall is the gate.

Fifty feet below, a praying Jew takes shelter from the rain in a gateway leading to Wilson's Arch.

One of several excavated passages adjacent to the Wall leading to the Hasmonian Tunnel.

The place is the site of a huge reunion. It is a reunion of Jews with other Jews, a reunion with their history and their past, even with their dead. And, as with all reunions, many of them are personal.

If you compare this place to the Kaaba in Mecca or to St. Peter's Square in the Vatican, you won't have the feeling of solemnity and awe of tens of thousands of kneeling and praying and singing people. There is no centrality in the Jewish religion and no central authority like the pope in the Catholic church. Everyday life goes together with

the divine. One of the many names of God is "Place." Just "The Place." So-called Lower (physical Earth) "Jerusalem" and so-called Upper (heavenly/spiritual) Jerusalem are together. There is a division between men and women at the Wall, but there is no division between Holy, Holy, Holy and Hello, Hello, Hello. There are no saints and no miracles at this place. The only irrational behavior and cultic activity is putting pledges and requests between the stones. These pieces of paper have mostly very personal requests written on them. Lately, there have been warnings about these papers endangering the stability of the Wall itself. And yet again, down to reality, these pieces of paper seem like the submission of questionnaires to some strange administration. God here is both very private and personal and very communal and universal.

Many ancient cultic buildings are well kept in their beauty, as in Egypt, Greece, or Mexico. Tourists flock there to be impressed by past human culture. Architects, when rebuilding or restoring an old monument, always leave a small part of the original—a few square yards of the old wall or pieces of the old doors and windows— untouched. All over the world, half-destroyed buildings are well preserved by authorities. We have the ruins in Auschwitz, Hiroshima, and Coventry, to mention just three. People come there to remember and to pray that those terrible events will never happen again.

Like these mute witnesses, the Western Wall is a memorial and warning. But it is much more. In Jerusalem, most holy sites may not be what they pretend to be. So it is with King David's tomb and other holy graves.

The wall under Wilson's Arch, which was the Herodian bridge connecting the upper city with the Temple Mount.

The Western Wall is what it always was. In the Jewish religion, there is always memory. There is an expression, "memory of the destruction," that is always acted out in symbolic rituals. One of them is the famous and popular breaking of a glass under the feet of the bridegroom at the wedding ceremony. It is not a superstition that broken glass brings good luck, it is the memory of the destruction of the Temple.

A few weeks ago, I was sitting in the late afternoon on the roof terrace of the Safdies in the Old City. This terrace overlooks the Western Wall plaza, most of the Old City, and Mount Scopus and the Mount of Olives. We were all seated in comfortable chairs and I felt as if I were sitting in a grandstand overlooking what seemed to be the greatest theater show in history. I could point out dozens of buildings and sights and to relate with them events that happened in the past, but also point into the future. That is what great drama always achieves.

It was from this same roof terrace that many of these photographs were taken, this same terrace view that inspired the artist to do this book. Like all spectacular sites, people always tell you to see this place at sunset. You must see it at sunrise, you must see it in the rain, or in early spring or at midnight. So I went to the Wall on the ninth of Av when Jews fast and mourn the destruction of the Temple. I noticed that the whole place was turned into a home where someone had died and friends and family came for condolence visits. And again I had this double vision: the Wall is the one who mourns and people come to comfort it; and the people on the plaza are the bereaved family with the Wall consoling and trying to comfort them. As I was sitting on the roof terrace, I had a few more ideas and variations of the Wall. Everyone needs a Wall like this in life. To lean on it, and weep and laugh, and to get comfort, to kiss it, and to hit it with your fists. Every wall can serve as a Western Wall. The Wall is never alone and we are never alone. I also thought about the common saying, "talking to the wall." This Wall is listening and sometimes even has an answer.

I also viewed the Wall itself again and again. I saw the layers of stones. The big stones from the time of the Temples, and the smaller, more recent stones, and the top invisible layer goes up into space and eternity and could be God.

And then I thought that the Western Wall is like the black box remaining after a catastrophic crash. And we might never be able to open it to get the answers to history. So we just let it be closed there as a reminder.

There are two situations for worship and prayer. One is from below (*de profundis*) and the other is from above. The artist has taken her pictures from below, among the people and stones, and from above. One of the photographs from above has Jews praying on one side and Moslems kneeling on the other side of the Wall. They seem to be on the same level, and their equality is the equality of God and may be a glimpse of hopeful peace.

And, finally, this book is not a tourist album. This is almost like a picture prayer book.

YEHUDA AMICHAI

FROM THE PHOTOGRAPHER

SINCE JUNE 1967, when Jerusalem was reunited, the Western Wall has been totally transformed.

For hundreds of years, the Wall was almost hidden in a cul-de-sac, seen only within a confined space, and never from a distance. The demolition of the buildings in front of the praying area created a vast, uncontained plaza. From a place of prayer and memory used by individuals, it became a place of mass assembly as well. What had once been a site of primarily religious significance became a focal point of national life.

A great diversity of people converge at the Western Wall each day. They come from different places and for different reasons, each relating to the Wall in his or her own unique way. Observing the Wall and its visitors, roaming the plaza for day after day, season after season, I felt as if I was in the midst of a giant melting pot of ethnic groups, customs, religions, rites of passage, political events, tensions, loves, and memories. I soon realized the plaza acted as a microcosm of the many facets of life in Israel and in Jerusalem.

Before sunrise, as the city awakens, many gather for the morning prayer. On Monday and Thursday mornings multiple bar mitzvah ceremonies are performed side by side, attracting celebrating families from around the

One of the few Arab homes left facing the Wall.

country and the world. During this time, one can observe the different traditions and customs of the diverse ethnic groups. As the sun swings toward the south, casting shadows of the vegetation sprouting from the Wall, tourists arrive in large groups, led by flag-waving guides wearing orange, white, or yellow colored hats. Some stand at a distance while others touch the Wall and place a written wish between its large stones. On certain days, as the afternoon sets in, workers set up hundreds of chairs and platforms for the swearing-in of an army platoon, or a mass prayer celebration, or a protest. At sunset, as the Wall changes its color to orange-gold and long shadows are cast by the bodies of those praying, brides and grooms arrive for a photo and video opportunity. As night falls, large groups of black-robed Hasidic Jews often descend for a special prayer or celebration.

And then there is the seasonal cycle. Before Rosh Hashanah and Yom Kippur, early morning prayer mixed with the trumpetlike sounding of the shofar attracts pilgrims from all parts of the country. On the ninth day of Av, the day of remembering the destruction of the Temple, tens of thousands gather and sleep along the Wall (the only time when this is permitted). During Passover, Shavuout, and Sukkot, the three traditional times of pilgrimage, thousands descend on Jerusalem to celebrate and worship. All this goes on, rain or shine, day or night. The Wall is never left alone. Nor is there a moment of darkness. As the sun sets, floodlights are turned on, creating a harsh glow in the heart of the Old City.

At first, I would record these moments from my terrace. But as time went by, I descended and mingled among the crowd to capture moments in the life of this or that person. Making this transition from the relative detachment of photographing from a distance through a long lens to the fast heartbeat of close-up contact was not easy. It was as if I was participating in a private moment of prayer, celebration, happiness, or despair. Already exposed in the vastness of the unsheltered plaza and fearing to intrude, I would often retreat if observed, and continue to photograph unnoticed. Nevertheless, both per-

Michal Ronnen Safdie, 1968, age 16, partaking in an archaeological excavation led by Professor Benjamin Mazar, on the southern side of the Wall, taken shortly after the unification of the city. Photograph by Werner Braun.

spectives were necessary in order to capture the many "stories of the Wall."

Contrasting emotions could be seen clearly on each roll of film. Several frames might show a bride and groom being videotaped as they looked toward a new future, followed by a sequence of frames focusing on a child afflicted with cancer brought by parents to the Wall to pray for a miraculous healing. There were other special moments, such as when Moslem prayers coincided with those of Jews. During the Ramadan, Friday noon prayers take place on the grounds of the Temple Mount which is covered like a carpet with devout, kneeling Moslems: women around the Golden Dome, and men under the pine trees toward the Al-Aqsa mosque. Simultaneously, fifty feet below, at the base of the Wall the Jews pray. Neither group seems to be aware of the presence of the other; only at a distance and from above is this realized.

While there is a predictable cycle of events which drew me to the Wall and put me on alert, I had the added advantage of living directly across from the Wall. Facing east, situated on top of an escarpment in the Jewish Quarter, our home overlooks the Western Wall precinct, the Dome of the Rock, and the Al-Aqsa mosque with the backdrop of the Mount of Olives and its graveyard. To the southeast rise the bare Judean Mountains and those of Moab in Jordan.

The chant of the muezzin originating in the minaret of the mosque appears to emerge from the depths of the earth, rising upward toward the heavens. Often, this coincides with church bells in the Christian quarter and praying or chanting at the Wall. These mingling sounds are testimony to the presence of the three great religions in the city.

When the Western Wall is an integral part of your home, when it provides the commanding view from every window, nothing about daily life can be routine. A

View of the Wall from the photographer's living room.

constant awareness of the Wall prevails whether you are awake or asleep.

And so it happened that I was awakened in the middle of one night by chanting at the Wall. Rushing to the window, I thought I was still dreaming as this most moving and surrealistic moment of the Hasidim—holding hands and dancing in front of the brightly lit Wall set against the darkness of the city—unfolded in front of my eyes. Similarly on the ninth of Av, at the end of a full day of photographing at the Wall, as I called it a day and retired, I was soon awakened to discover that the colorful assembly of thousands during the day gave way to a tightly clustered group of black-robed Hasidim. Naturally, I grabbed my bags and ran down the narrow alley of the market to witness the group reorganize into three formal rows forming a "U" facing the Wall.

And so there were many times when I was called down to the Wall. I will never forget the moment when I was having breakfast with my family and noticed large groups of tourists arriving in the plaza, each with their own colored hats. By the time I reached the Wall there was a high-pitched hum, a sound not familiar to Jewish praying. Hundreds of Korean pilgrims had entered the women's praying area, pressing their bodies and hands against the Wall. It was the first time I had spotted men in the women's area. I felt as if I was in the midst of their trance, almost paralyzed myself. And then there were the moments I missed, such as when nuns dressed in white spread out at the women's praying area, like doves of peace. By the time I reached them they had left the Wall and were gathered in the plaza.

Since men and women are separated at the immediate praying area, I was restricted to photographing men from a distance. This meant I could neither choose an angle, compose a frame, nor follow a moment that might have been of interest. The only time I could try to get closer was during a bar mitzvah, the only time women are permitted to stand on chairs and look over the partition. So I resorted to using a very long lens or simply attaching a telescope to the camera. Those moments captured through the telescope actually give the sense of peeking through a hole in a door.

David's City in the foreground as it appears today outside the Ottoman City Wall built by Suleiman the Magnificent in c. 1540. In the center is the Temple Mount with the two mosques, and the Western Wall is seen at center left.

At the end of my year of photographing within and around the plaza, it seemed appropriate to try to place the Wall within the larger context of the city. I was born in Jerusalem forty-five years ago, but I had never flown over it and did not anticipate the depth of emotion I would feel as I approached the city by helicopter from the north with the sun about to set. While trying to reassure myself that I would not fall out of my seat or drop one of the lenses, the entire city surrounded by the Old City Wall rising from the Judean desert was there for me to capture. It was as if three thousand years of history were unfolding in front of my eyes, erasing any present boundaries between religions, Arabs and Jews, secular and religious, past and present.

As the pilot moved in towards the Wall, just like a zoom lens, constantly coming in closer and moving back, we reached the perfect angle. I realized that this is what I had been doing the entire year, moving the lens from between the crevices of the Wall to the complexity of situations and emotions around it. What I wished to convey were the sounds, the hum of praying, the voices of the awakening city, their joyous singing or painful cry. As the pilot pulled back, I reflected on how fortunate I was to be able to tell this story to others.

This book would not have come to being without the personal commitment and support of Hugh Levin. He personally guided the entire conception and production, putting together a remarkable team: Ellin Yassky Silberblatt, my editor, who not only conducted us firmly and gently, but enriched this book with her own perspective; Philip Grushkin, whose sensitive design respected each photograph and brought endless new ideas to their presentation. Most of all, I am grateful for the patience and respect given to my own desires and wishes. This was true and pleasurable teamwork. I am indebted to Dorothy Harman, my agent-friend, whose involvement and support exceeded beyond the call of duty.

My respect and gratitude go to Yehuda Amichai who amplified the photographs by reaching into the soul of the city and its history. My appreciation goes also to Panorama Colour Labs Ltd. Jerusalem who developed and printed most of the images, and particularly to Monica Katzman.

I am most grateful to my friends Martin Peretz and Nitza Rosovsky who shared not only professional knowledge but spent time helping to push this project forward. My thanks to Suri Drucker who coordinated and organized with enthusiasm many aspects of the project. My appreciation to my father who actually conceived the idea of creating a book after seeing the first collection of photographs, and my mother, who showered me with practical and emotional support. Keren, my sister, patiently reviewed each photograph at every stage of my work. My daughters Yasmin and Carmelle lived with this project every day for the past two years. They endured many late meals and interrupted conversations as I would often unexpectedly rush down to the Wall.

I am most grateful to my husband and best friend, Moshe, who created the conditions for my development as a photographer in the first place. His love, patience, and constructive criticism always pushed me a step forward, his eye enriched my own, and his presence is felt in every image and word of this book.

MICHAL RONNEN SAFDIE

Holy,
Holy,
Holy —
Hello,
Hello,
Hello

*Hasidic Jews on the
first day of Passover.*

Nuns overlooking the Wall.

Catholic nun on a visit to the Wall.

These older women can be seen daily at the Wall.
Many come to beg alms.

Two Ethiopian Jews, recently emigrated to Israel, leave the plaza on the ninth of Av.

A group of visitors to the Wall take shelter from the midday sun under their umbrellas.

Brightly-colored umbrellas mark leaders of the Jewish Ethiopian community.

An American dancer, working on a cruise ship docked in Haifa, visits the Wall.

A school visit during the Shavuot holiday.

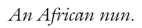

An African nun.

OPPOSITE:

A bride and groom partaking in the ritual of pre-wedding photography.

54

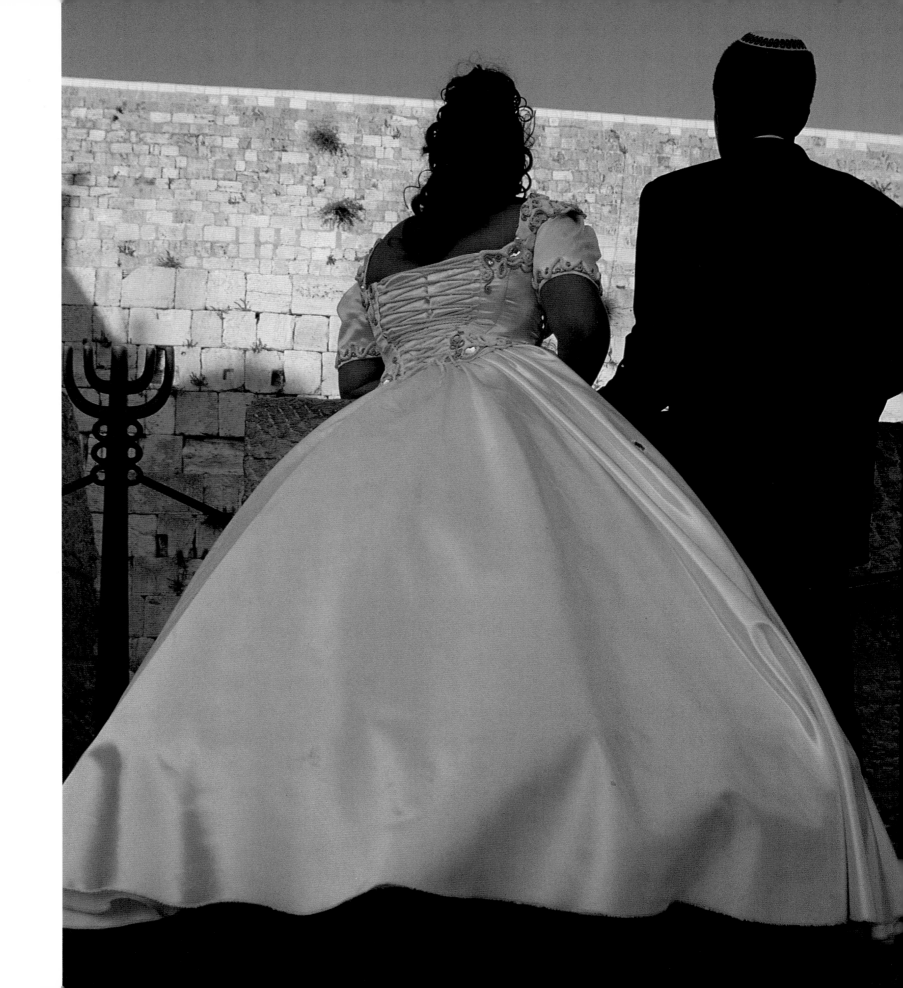

A partially blind Moslem passing by a security checkpoint following a Friday prayer at the Al-Aqsa mosque.

OPPOSITE:

Ending their several-day hike, Israeli soldiers arrive at the Wall for an initiation ceremony.

56

A tourist being wheeled in a merchandise cart, generally used in the narrow alleys of the Old City.

These infirmed are brought to the Wall courtesy of Yad Sara, who provide for the elderly.

Cancer afflicted summer campers visit the Wall guided by staff for a prayer of healing.

*A concentration
camp survivor.*

An Ethiopian Israeli.

A Site
of
Huge
Reunion

*A mass prayer and protest following
a series of terrorist attacks.*

Early morning activities during the Days of Awe
(the days between Rosh Hashanah and Yom Kippur).

Awakening at the Wall on the ninth of Av.

Midnight on the ninth of Av.

4:00 A.M. *Hasidic Jews.*

Two Bukharan families arrive for bar mitzvah celebrations.

Mourning the destruction of the Temple on the ninth of Av, visitors sit on the ground as is customary during the Shiva period.

79

A giant banner shows the Brooklyn home of the late Lubavitcher Rabbi, Menahem Mendel Schneirson, as a backdrop for a mass bar and bat mitzvah of 1000 boys and girls seen at right. Seated above, are the two chief rabbis of Israel.

Sukkot celebrations in which the four ceremonial species (arba minim) are held.

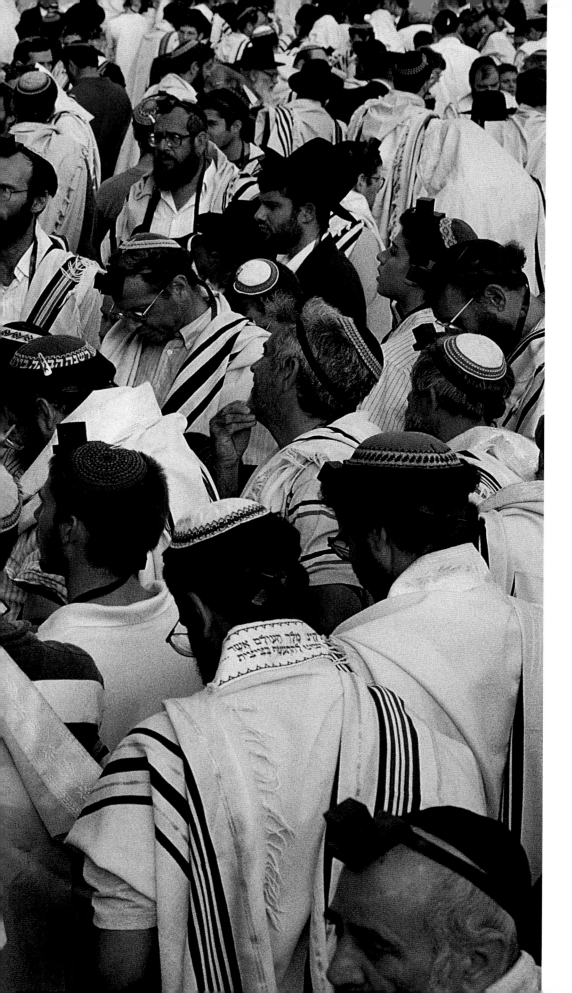

Afternoon prayers on the ninth of Av.

During the days between Rosh Hashanah and Yom Kippur, an Israeli boy of Hungarian/Indian descent comes to Jerusalem.

*Memorial Day
ceremonies
remembering
the fallen
in Israel's wars.*

God Seekers, Hope Seekers, Peace Seekers

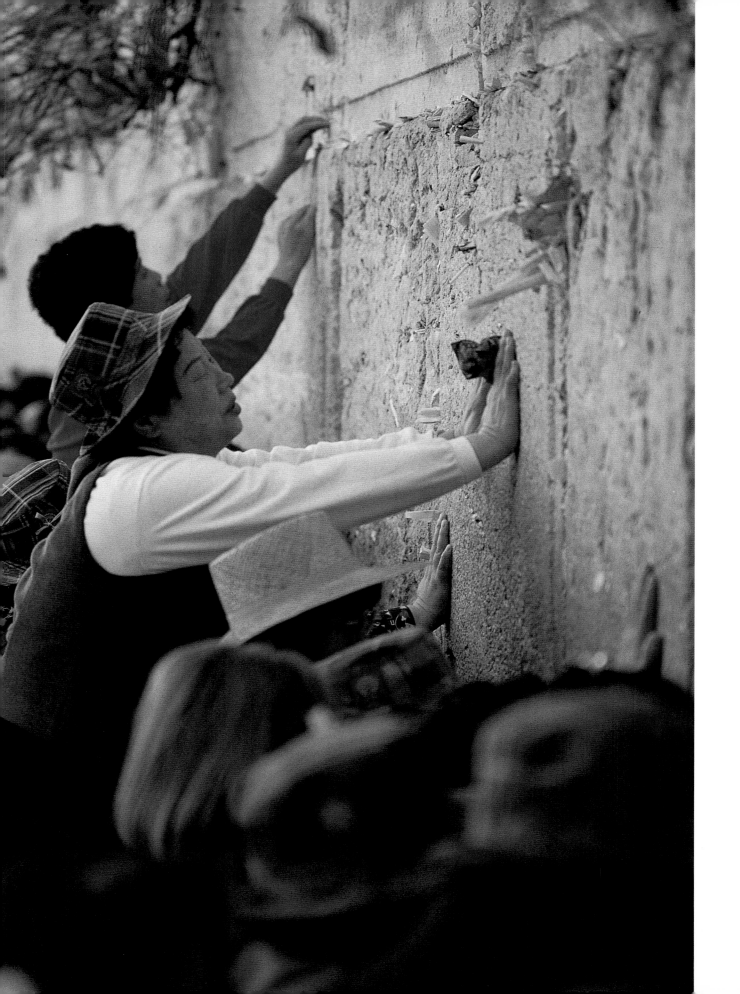

*Members of a Korean
sect on a pilgrimage to
the Wall.*

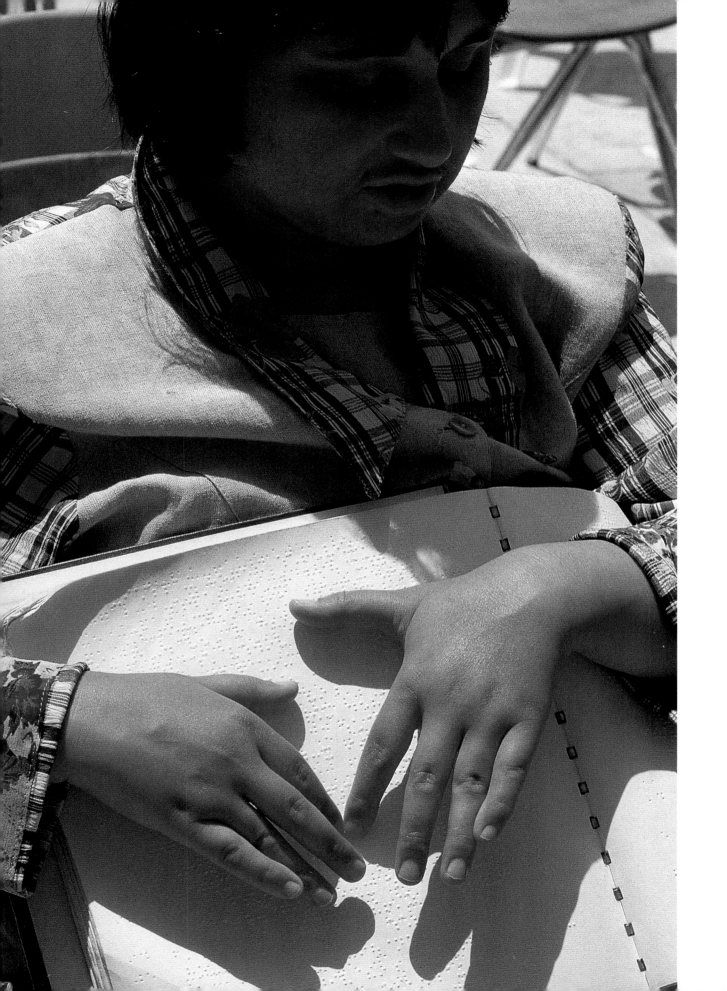

*An interlude from Air Force
pilot flight training.*

The women's section on a rainy day.

End of the day clean up.

Soul
Language,
Body
Language,
Stone
Language

Giant banner of the late
Rabbi Menahem Mendel
Schneirson, perceived to be
the Messiah by many of his
followers in the Lubavitcher
community. This banner
is a backdrop to a mass bar
mitzvah ceremony for
newly arrived immigrants.

An Italian nun stands in front of a poster proclaiming "Prepare for the Coming of the Messiah," sponsored by the Lubavitch.

Prayers during Yom Kippur.

An early morning visit by a group of Italian nuns.